TECHNOLOGY IN ACTION

INFORMATION TECHNOLOGY

Mark Lambert

Wayland

Titles in this series

First published in 1990 by
Wayland (Publishers) Ltd
61 Western Road, Hove
East Sussex BN3 1JD, England

©Copyright 1990 Wayland (Publishers) Ltd

Edited by Roger Coote
Designed by David Armitage

Front cover Microcomputers are playing an increasingly important part in the growth of information technology in schools and homes.

British Library Cataloguing in Publication Data
Lambert, Mark, *1946-*
    Information technology
    1. Information systems
    I. Title. II. Series
    303.4833

    ISBN 1-85210-788-X

Typeset by Direct Image Photosetting Limited,
Sussex, England
Printed in Italy by G. Canale & C.S.p.A., Turin
Bound in France by A.G.M.

Contents

Information is an essential part of our lives. From the time we are born we begin to acquire information about the world around us. Ever since then our store of information has been added to from many different sources – our parents, teachers, radio and television programmes, magazines and books. This book is adding a little bit more to your own store of knowledge.

One of the things that sets humans apart from other animals is the ability to reason. We use our knowledge and understanding of the world to work out new ideas, which are then added to our store of information. Facts are obviously vital to this reasoning process. However, no one person can memorize all human knowledge so, over the last few thousand years, people have developed methods of storing facts and ideas, and for passing such information from one person to another. Today, we refer to the sophisticated methods we use to achieve this as information technology, or IT.

The origins of information technology go back to earliest human times. The use of spoken language, for example, began very early in human history, probably over half a million

Satellites such as this Tracking and Data Relay Satellite (TDRS) are an essential part of the modern communications industry.

Above Computer technology is vital to modern business. Here stockbrokers in London are using computers to keep track of the changing prices of stocks and shares.

years ago. About 30,000 years ago people began to record things in the form of drawings on the walls of caves. Then picture languages, or hieroglyphics, were developed and they eventually evolved into alphabets. For the first time, information could be stored permanently in a written form.

Important milestones in the development of information technology include the invention of the printing press in about 1450, the electric telegraph in 1837, the telephone in 1876, radio communications in the early 1900s, television in the 1920s and communications satellites in the 1960s. Gradually, the transfer of information has been speeded up. Storing information became much easier with the development of efficient electronic computers during the 1950s and 1960s. Today, electronic devices play a crucial role in the storage and communication of information.

Below About 5,000 years ago the Egyptians stored information in the form of a picture language that developed into a system of symbols known as hieroglyphics.

Sending messages from one place to another used to be a slow process. They generally had to be carried by human messengers travelling on foot or on horseback. Simple messages could sometimes be sent using beacons (bonfires), and during the late eighteenth century people began using a form of visual telegraph – semaphore towers with arms that could be moved to indicate different letters of the alphabet or even phrases. However, in foggy or misty conditions such visual signals were impossible to see.

In the eighteenth century, a semaphore tower was a convenient device for sending messages from a shore-based signalling station to ships.

During the late eighteenth and early nineteenth centuries several inventors attempted to build an electric telegraph. This early experiment, in about 1774, by Frenchman Georges-Louis Lessage used 24 wires, each one representing a different letter of the alphabet.

Signalling was speeded up by the invention of the electric telegraph. The first telegraphic devices appeared in Europe and the USA in the early 1800s. Francisco Salva of Barcelona devised a machine that used 26 wires to send messages, one for each letter of the alphabet. The British inventors Charles Wheatstone and William Cooke built a machine that used only five wires. Then in 1838 the American Samuel Morse patented his idea for using a system of short and long signals – 'dots and dashes' – known as Morse code, that could be sent along a single wire.

Morse's system was adopted all over the world and during the 1850s an international network of telegraph lines began to appear. In 1866 a cable was even laid across the Atlantic Ocean. At first signals had to be coded and decoded by operators, which slowed down the process. Then, in 1855 David Hughes, an English scientist working in the USA, invented a printing telegraph machine that operated like a typewriter and automatically coded and decoded messages.

During the late nineteenth century the telephone (see page 11) began to replace the telegraph. However, two new forms of telegraph were introduced during the early twentieth century by the telephone companies themselves. In 1907 the first facsimile (now known as 'fax') transmission was sent – a London newspaper received a copy of a photograph from Paris. During the 1930s telephone companies introduced a teletypewriter service that telephone subscribers could use to send printed messages to each other. Known as telex in the UK and TWX in the USA, these systems are still widely used today. The most modern form of telex, known as supertelex or teletex, is designed to work with computers. Using supertelex, it is possible to transmit 3,000 characters in just 10 seconds – an ordinary telex system takes more than twenty times as long to do this.

Telephone and telegraph messages have to be sent along wires. During the late nineteenth century several scientists began to look for a way of sending messages without using wires. The most successful was the Italian engineer Guglielmo Marconi. In 1901 he succeeded in sending a wireless signal from Cornwall in Britain to Newfoundland in Canada, using radio waves. The discovery of how to use radio waves to carry signals opened the way for a new era of technology.

In a modern telex machine, the message to be sent can be composed on a screen before being transmitted. Incoming messages are printed out.

Guglielmo Marconi with some of the apparatus he used to transmit early wireless signals.

To begin with, radio signals were sent using Morse code. However, by this time the technology needed to turn sound into electricity, and vice versa, was being developed for use in telephones and gramophones. In addition, scientists had invented several very useful electronic devices. One of these, the diode (two-electrode) valve, was invented by the English scientist John Fleming in 1904 for detecting radio signals. The triode (three- electrode) valve, invented by the American Lee de Forest in 1906, could be used to increase the strength of, or amplify, the signals. Later, in 1906, as a result of these inventions, Reginald Fessenden, another American scientist, built a radio transmitter that could send speech. His transmitter broadcast a continuous 'carrier' radio wave that was modulated, or made to vary, by electrical signals produced by speech and music. At the receiver the signal was demodulated – that is, the carrier wave was removed leaving only the sound signal that it carried.

Modern televisions are equipped with push-button digital technology and can be operated by remote control.

Radio technology continued to improve. In 1918 Edwin Armstrong, an officer in the US Army, invented a device known as the super-heterodyne receiver. It enabled radio sets to become more sensitive to weak signals and better at tuning in to individual radio stations. This device still forms an important part of a modern radio set.

During the 1920s a number of scientists and inventors began looking for ways to use radio waves to transmit pictures as well as sound. An electronic device known as the cathode ray tube had been invented in 1897 by the German scientist Ferdinand Braun. This led to the development of the electronic picture tube and camera. The first all-electronic television system was developed by the Russian-born scientist Vladimir Zworykin in the 1930s. Since then technological innovation has steadily improved television systems. Modern television pictures are of very high quality and many TVs now have a range of sophisticated features such as stereophonic sound and computerized information (see page 21).

The telephone is such an important part of most people's everyday lives that it is hard to imagine how the world managed without it. Yet this instrument has only existed for just over 100 years and it is only in the last 50 years that making a telephone call has become so easy.

The telephone was invented by an American, Alexander Graham Bell. In 1875, while working on a telegraph device intended to transmit several messages at the same time, he discovered that sounds could be transmitted electrically along a wire. One year later he succeeded in sending recognizable words, and in 1878 the first telephone exchange opened in the USA.

Over the years a variety of technological innovations have helped to improve the telephone. Bell's system used a combined microphone and earpiece, which made talking and listening rather difficult. In 1877 another famous American inventor, Thomas Alva Edison, devised a separate mouthpiece and earpiece.

The development of the telephone enabled people to communicate more easily over long distances.

During the early twentieth century this telephone exchange at the Paris Opera enabled callers to listen to performances over the telephone.

At first all calls had to be connected by an operator, but in 1889 Almon Strowger invented an automatic telephone exchange. Local numbers could be called by pressing buttons (which were soon replaced by a rotating dial).

Long-distance telephone calls only became possible with the invention of a boosting device. A number of these devices placed at 1-km intervals along a telephone line enabled signals to be carried over any distance.

Telephone exchanges were improved in the late 1930s with the introduction of a new type of switch, called the crossbar switch. It was faster than the Strowger switch and enabled the exchange to carry a greater number of calls at the same time. Electronically controlled exchanges were introduced during the 1960s and became more sophisticated in the 1980s. Analogue systems, in which signals are sent as varying electric currents, are now being replaced by digital systems, in which the signals are transmitted as a series of pulses that can be read by a computer. It is this digital technology that has given us today's push-button, rapid-dialling telephones equipped with silicon chip memories. Long distance calls are now routed via optical fibre cables (see page 22) and microwave links.

Digital technology has allowed telephone companies to introduce a range of new services. People can use information services to find out such things as the exact time, the weather forecast, sports results and share prices. It is also possible to dial into a 'party' line on which up to ten people can chat together at the same time. Business people can use a similar facility to set up conferences over the telephone.

In recent years facsimile transmission has become easier and faster. As a result it has also become increasingly popular and many companies now use 'fax' machines to send copies of letters, reports, diagrams and photographs. The document to be sent is scanned electronically, using a beam of light and a sensor that measures the amount of light reflected from each part of the document. This information is translated into an electrical signal that is sent via the telephone system to another fax machine, which decodes the signal and prints a copy of the original document.

Above A technician inspecting one of the circuit boards in a modern digital telephone exchange.

Below A facsimile machine has become an essential feature of a modern office.

A mobile phone allows a busy executive to keep in touch with clients at all times.

Another recent innovation is the portable telephone, which is a result of combining telephone technology and radio. The simplest is the domestic cordless telephone in which the cable that normally connects the telephone to the handset is replaced by a radio link.

This type of portable telephone operates over a very short range – up to a hundred metres or so from the telephone base. Truly mobile systems rely on more powerful radio signals and can be used anywhere. Mobile car telephones have been in use since the 1970s, but early equipment tended to be bulky and the number of radio frequencies available was limited.

During the 1980s, however, a system known as cellular radio was introduced. The country is divided up into a series of interlocking, hexagonal areas, or cells, each of which has its own radio transmitter/receiver. This system makes it possible to use the same frequencies in different cells, provided that the cells are not next door to each other, and thus many more people can now use mobile telephones. At the same time digital technology and miniaturization of components have made it possible to produce very small portable telephones that can be carried in a coat pocket and used anywhere within the cellular radio system.

Silicon chips are now a normal part of our everyday lives. The digital watch on your wrist, your electronic calculator, the computers you use, and the television and digital telephone in your home all contain these marvels of modern electronic engineering. They can also be found in cars, cameras, burglar alarms and fire detection systems. In fact, the silicon chip is the basis of all today's information technology.

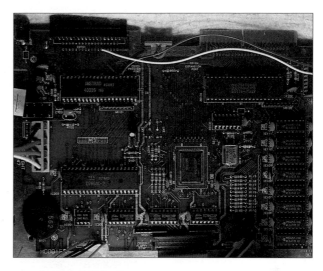

Right Silicon chips form the basis of modern computer technology. Attached to this computer circuit board are microprocessor and memory chips in their protective cases, together with other electronic components.

Below The introduction of the electronic calculator was made possible by the development of silicon chips. A digital watch also contains a silicon chip and the calculator shown here has a built-in stopwatch and alarm.

The story of the silicon chip goes back to the discovery of materials known as semi-conductors. Conductors are materials, mostly metals, that allow electricity to flow through them. Non-conductors are materials like plastics and ceramics that do not allow electricity to flow. Semiconductors are materials that conduct electricity about a thousand million times better than non-conductors, but a thousand million times less well than conductors. Their structure is basically like that of non-conductors, but under certain conditions they will allow very small electric currents to flow.

Semiconductors were first investigated during the 1940s by William Shockley. For many years it had been known that certain crystals could be used as diodes, or rectifiers, to convert alternating electric current into direct current.

Shockley discovered that a small piece of a crystal called germanium containing a tiny amount of impurity acted as an even better diode. Then in 1947, working with two other scientists, John Bardeen and Walter Brattain, he found a way of combining semiconductor diodes to make a triode. They named this device a transistor, because it seemed to transfer electric current across a resistor.

The transistor revolutionized radio, television and computer technology. These had previously relied on valves which tended to burn out. Transistors, on the other hand, were small and capable of working reliably for many years. Valves soon became a thing of the past, and scientists began to discover other semi-conductor materials. The most widely used today is silicon.

Attaching the tiny external wire connections to a silicon chip is a very delicate task that must be carried out in completely dust-free conditions. When they are in position, the wires are automatically soldered into place.

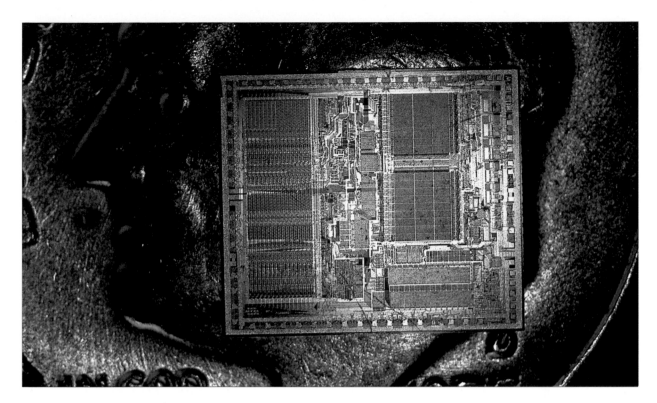

This Motorola microprocessor chip, seen on the surface of a US dime coin, contains the equivalent of about 70,000 transistors.

Early computers were extremely large and, by today's standards, not very powerful. Using transistors instead of valves made it possible for the computers of the 1950s to be smaller, more powerful and more reliable. Similar improvements occurred in radios and televisions. Then, in 1958, an American company, Texas Instruments, produced a device they called the integrated circuit. Basically, this consists of a very small slice of silicon on which are placed a variety of electronic components – transistors, diodes, resistors and capacitors – connected together with microscopic threads of metal. The integrated circuit soon became popularly known as the silicon chip, or microchip.

Since then, the number of electronic components that can be placed on a chip has increased dramatically; today, it is possible to put several thousand on a slice of silicon smaller than a fingernail. Until recently a microprocessor chip was described as a silicon chip containing all of the components needed to make the central processing unit of a computer. However, in 1989 the American chip manufacturer Intel produced a 'superchip' that contains not only a central processing unit but also a memory and a graphics unit. The chip measures 10 cm by 15 cm and contains 1 million transistors. In 1990 Intel's main rival, Motorola, announced that they had produced a chip measuring 14 cm square with 4 million transistors crammed on to its surface.

Silicon chips are used for many different purposes. A digital telephone, for example, contains a chip that translates analogue signals into digital signals, and vice versa. Many telephones also have memory chips for storing numbers and control chips for automatic dialling. Some telephones have a liquid crystal display (LCD) screen that is controlled by another chip. Messages can also be recorded on memory chips and replayed by a speech synthesizer chip. A microprocessor chip is needed to control and co-ordinate all of these chips.

Thirty years ago computers were so large that they each occupied a large room, and so complicated to operate that expert technicians were needed. Today, there are more powerful computers that fit easily on to a table or desk, or even on a person's lap, and can be operated by anyone who can understand a simple set of instructions. The computer is a tool and, as with any other tool, the operator only needs to understand what it will do and how to make it work – not exactly *how* it works.

Computers are a vital part of the modern world. They have become as important to us as as the plough, the internal combustion engine and the radio. People who live in the technologically advanced countries of the world would now find life very much more difficult without computers.

The origins of the computer go back to the abacus, first used over 5,000 years ago. During the seventeenth and nineteenth centuries, several mechanical calculating machines were devised. However, the first successful computer was an electronic machine called ENIAC (Electronic Numerical Integrator and Calculator), built in the USA in 1946. It was huge, occupying a total volume of 760 cubic metres and using nearly 18,000 triode valves. During the next five years several electronic computers were built in America and Britain, among them MANIAC (Mathematical Analyser, Numerator, Integrator and Computer) and UNIVAC (Universal Automatic Computer), which was the first machine to be programmed (given instructions) with information on magnetic tape instead of on punched tape or cards.

ENIAC, the first electronic computer, occupied a large room. One of its early achievements was to solve in two hours a problem in nuclear physics that would otherwise have taken 100 engineers a whole year to work out. However, a modern mainframe computer could solve the same problem in just a few seconds.

Above The Cray-2 supercomputer at Lawrence Livermore Laboratory in California, USA, is used to carry out the calculations involved in research into laser fusion and laser weapons.

Below A battery-powered lap-top microcomputer can be used almost anywhere.

During the 1950s computers, equipped with transistors instead of valves, became smaller. Businesses began using them for storing information and keeping accounts, but they were still fairly bulky and expensive. In 1960 a business computer occupied a large room and cost about £100,000 to install. Ten years later, as a result of the development of the silicon chip, a computer of equivalent calculating power could be housed in one corner of the same room and cost a mere £10,000. Desktop computers appeared in the late 1970s and, today, a desktop computer that can process the same amount of information as a 1960s office computer costs only a few hundred pounds.

Speed and power are the main concerns of today's computer designers. The largest modern computers have truly staggering processing powers. A Cray-2 supercomputer contains over 200,000 silicon chips and can handle several billion calculations each second. In doing so it generates a great deal of heat and its circuit boards have to be bathed in a liquid called Fluorinert in order to keep them cool.

19

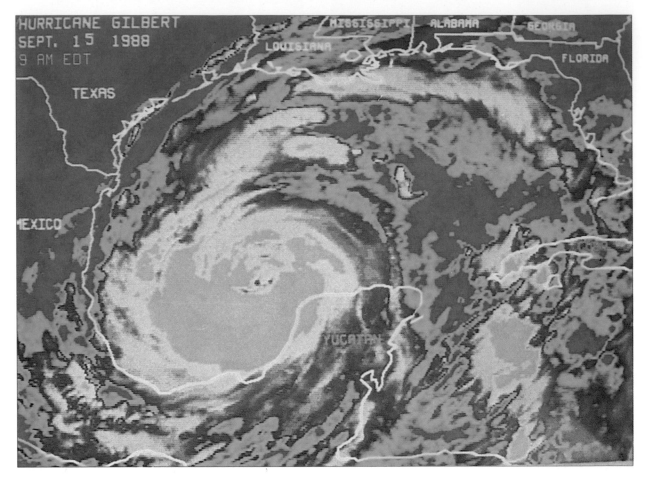

A computer image, created from information received from a satellite, of Hurricane
Gilbert, which swept across the Caribbean and the Gulf of Mexico in September 1988.

Such computers are used to process information for such things as the NASA space
shuttle and worldwide weather forecasts,
where an enormous amount of data and many
complex calculations are involved.

Future supercomputers will use parallel processing, in which several calculations are per-
formed at the same time instead of one after the
other, as they are at present. Meanwhile computer networks (see page 38) are now replacing
single mainframe computers, and optical discs
(see page 25) are beginning to be used in place
of magnetic storage devices.

Computers can be used for an enormous
variety of different purposes, according to the
way they are programmed. Some are used as
high-speed calculating machines, in such areas

as space technology, scientific research and
weather forecasting. They can also be used for
what is called computer-aided design, or CAD,
in which sophisticated modern graphics programs enable calculations to be expressed as
graphs and drawings on a video screen.
Graphics programs are also used to create
spectacular images for use in computer games
programs.

Alternatively, a computer can be made to
behave like a very versatile typewriter, by giving
it a word processor program. Or it can simply be
used as an information store, or databank. The
advantage of such a store is that the information
is easy to extract. A few key words can be used to
tell the computer to find the information in its
memory and display it on a screen.

Computers can also be linked into communications systems in order to transfer information from place to place. The two best-known computer information systems are teletext and viewdata. Teletext is computer information stored by television companies and broadcast along with normal programmes. Anyone with a suitable decoder can display the broadcast data on their television screen. Viewdata systems are often used by organizations, such as travel agents, banks, stockbrokers and airlines.

They pay a fee to the organization controlling the computer database and use the telephone system and a computer screen to gain access to the information. Anyone with a personal computer and a modem can use such databases. A modem is simply a device for connecting a computer to the telephone system. Communications operators, such as Telecom Gold in Britain, also use the telephone system to link owners of personal computers to databases, electronic 'noticeboards' and telex services.

In Britain the viewdata system known as Prestel is used by travel agents to check on the availability of such things as airline flights and hotel accommodation, and to make bookings for their customers.

The idea of using light to send messages is an old one. For thousands of years people have been sending coded messages using flashes of sunlight. During the last eighty years electric light has been used in much the same way. However, such signals can only be sent between people who can see each other and they are easily prevented by poor visibility. For most of this century electrical signals, using radio, telegraph and telephone systems, have proved to be more useful.

A metal wire, as in a telegraph or telephone, can only carry one signal at a time and so it takes two wires to carry a single conversation. Thus a cable capable of carrying, say, 6,000 conversations at once must have 12,000 wires, each of which has to be insulated from its neighbours. As a result, the cable is very thick and heavy.

Recently, this problem has been overcome by returning to the use of light. Scientists have developed ways of making fine optical fibres of very clear glass that can transmit light signals over long distances. Each fibre consists of two layers of glass – an inner core along which the light travels, and an outer cladding that prevents the light from passing out of the sides. Signals in neighbouring fibres do not affect each other and so the fibres do not need to be insulated, although they often have a plastic coating for protection. An optical fibre can also carry more than one beam of light, and each beam can carry more information than an electric current. As a result, a pair of optical fibres can carry over 1,900 telephone conversations and optical fibre cables can be made much smaller than conventional copper wire cables.

In an optical fibre, light travels down a central core. Little or no light escapes out of the sides and thus the intensity of the light is maintained along the fibre.

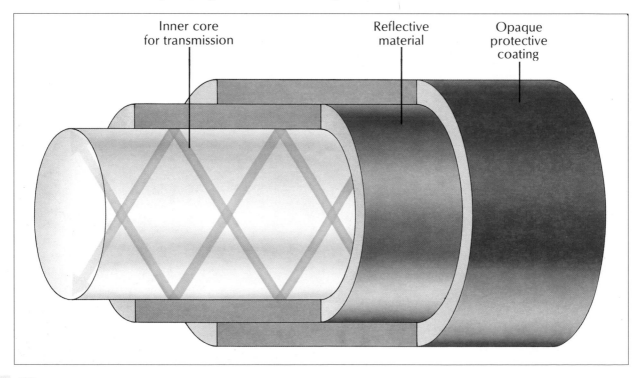

Inner core for transmission   Reflective material   Opaque protective coating

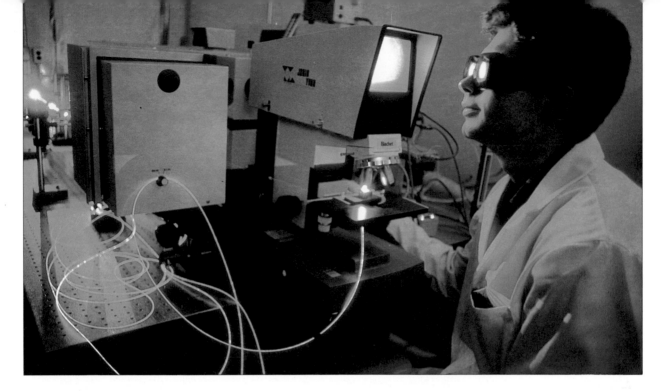

Above Optical fibres need to be of very high quality. Here, a technician at an optical fibre manufacturer is checking to see that the fibres being produced are of a high enough standard

In recent years the use of optical fibre cable has increased rapidly. In Britain over 750,000 km of the telephone network is now made up of optical fibre cable. In time engineers hope to be able to replace all copper cable with optical fibre cable, even inside people's homes. Trials are now taking place using optical fibres to carry a variety of other services, such as cable television, viewdata, a video library and hi-fi radio, which could all be brought into our homes through the same cables.

One of the first difficulties that had to be overcome during the development of optical fibres was finding a light source small enough to be directed easily into the end of such a fine fibre. In the early 1980s two possible light sources were being investigated. Small electronic devices known as light-emitting diodes (LEDs), then widely used in the displays of early digital watches and calculators, were tried. They were cheap and small but not very powerful and the light they produced needed to be amplified, or boosted, at frequent intervals along the length of the cable.

Below Optical fibres can be made so small that several could be passed through the eye of a sewing needle.

A photomicrograph of the surface of a compact disc, with part of the protective plastic layer removed to show the pits below. The picture was taken using a scanning electron microscope and colours have been added.

The alternative light source was the laser. This is a device that produces a narrow, powerful beam of very pure light that can be transmitted along an optical fibre over much greater distances than the light from an LED. Early lasers were rather large and expensive, but both of these drawbacks have now been overcome. Recently, scientists in the USA have succeeded in creating a silicon chip with an array of tiny lasers etched into its surface. Each laser is a cylinder about one-tenth of the thickness of a human hair, and over a million of these fit into each square centimetre of chip.

Fibre optic technology is currently the subject of much research. New lasers with better light-emitting properties are being developed, along with purer, clearer glass fibres that allow light to pass more easily.

Lasers are also being used in other ways, to help in the storage and retrieval of information. In the early 1980s sound and electronics engineers developed a way of using a laser to record digital information on the surface of a spinning disc. The information is recorded as a series of pits of varying length that represent the digital signals sent to the laser. The surface of the disc is coated with a highly reflective material and finally covered with a protective layer. The information can be 'read' using another laser to detect the pits. The signals from this laser are then translated back into the original signal.

This system was originally developed as a means of making high quality, permanent video recordings that could be played back on a television. Today, the most familiar form is the compact disc, which contains only sound recording. However, laser discs are also used to record computer information. Video discs, similar to the type originally designed, are also re-appearing, and engineers have recently developed a laser disc on which information can be recorded by the user.

A selection of compact discs. Many modern hi-fi systems include compact disc players.

Reading machines

Information can now be stored in a variety of forms. But in order to make use of such information we need machines that can read it and translate it into a form that we can understand.

Lasers can be used to read more than one form of stored information. In shops, for example, they are used to scan the computer bar codes that are now printed on many of the items we buy. At a checkout each bar code may be passed over a laser positioned under the counter. Alternatively, a laser 'pen' can be drawn rapidly across it. The laser beam is reflected back to a sensor that converts the light and dark bands of the code into a digital signal. This is interpreted as a stock number by the shop's computer, which automatically shows the price of the item on a display at the till, and records the fact that the shop now has one less of that item. This system makes stock control easier, and helps checkout queues move faster.

At a supermarket checkout, a laser beam scans the bar code on each item that is passed over a glass panel in the counter and the price is automatically recorded.

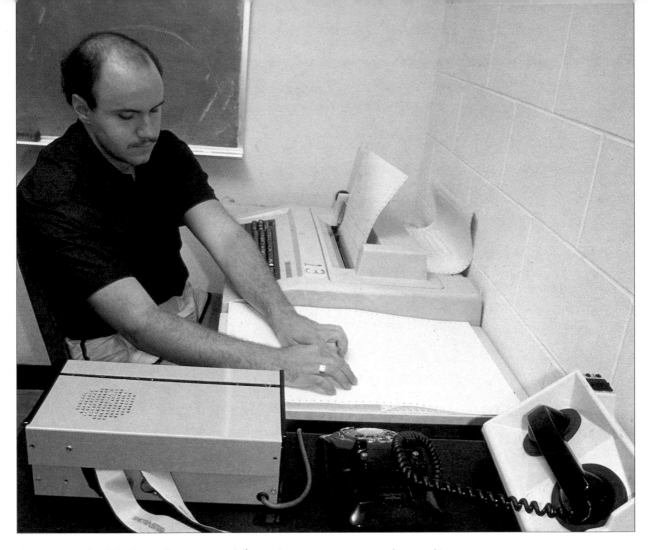

In order to give blind people access to information, a computer can be used to translate text into braille. The braille is produced by a special printer in the form of raised dots on paper.

Information can also be stored in the form of a magnetic pattern in a thin film of iron oxide. This is the principle used in tape recording and on several kinds of plastic card. The magnetic strip on a bank or credit card, for example, contains such information as the bank code number, the customer's name, account number and personal identity number (PIN), and the card's expiry date. When such a card is inserted into an appropriate machine, the magnetic information is converted into an electric signal by a reading head. Phonecards work in a similar way.

It is also possible for machines to read information printed on paper. A fax machine (see page 13) uses a beam of ordinary light to scan printed information. Some newspapers are scanned by laser beams and the digital information produced is then transmitted by satellite in order to speed up publication in far-off places.

Progress is also being made with machines that actually read individual characters and translate them into signals that can be recognized and stored by a computer. Some documents, such as cheques, are printed with special optical characters that computers can be programmed to read. There are also computers that can read ordinary printed text and scientists are trying to develop machines that can read handwriting.

The way in which we pay for goods has changed over the years. Originally people bartered, or exchanged goods, for the things that they needed. Some goods were more highly prized than others and became commonly used currencies. Early currencies included such things as cattle, rice grains, salt, cowrie shells and pieces of metal. Metal coins were first used some 3,000 years ago by the Chinese. Paper money, in the form of bank notes, also first appeared in China, during the seventh century AD. Bank cheques appeared in Europe and America early this century and credit cards first appeared in America during the 1920s.

Today, plastic credit and bank cards are equipped with machine-readable magnetic strips (see page 27). Such cards can be used to obtain money from bank cash dispensers and they are increasingly being used to pay for goods. A person purchasing a television, for

Above   A plastic bank card can be used at an automatic teller machine (ATM) to withdraw cash, check the balance of an account or order a statement.

Below   An EFTPOS (electronic funds transfer at point of sale) system can be made to transfer funds directly from a customer's bank account to the bank account of a shop by using a card with a magnetic strip. The process takes just a few seconds and no cash or cheques are needed.

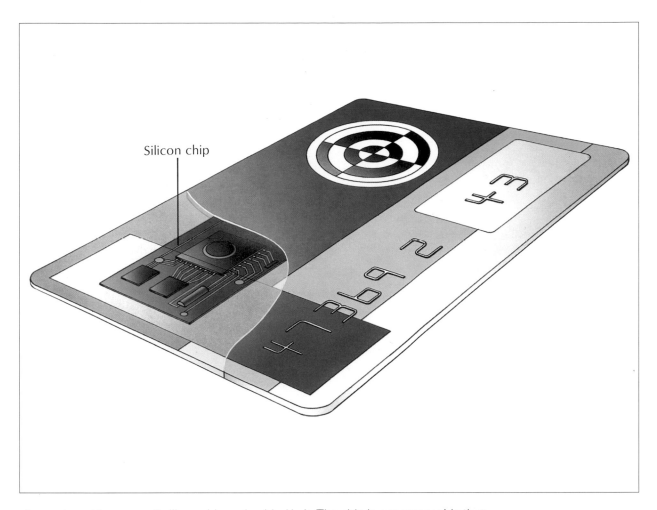

Silicon chip

A smart card has a small silicon chip embedded in it. The chip is a memory chip that keeps a record of all the transactions that the card is used for.

example, is asked to sign a small document that instructs the bank or credit card company to transfer the correct sum of money from his or her own account to the shop's account. In practice, of course, no money actually changes hands. The transaction is simply recorded in the computers of the banks involved.

Some shops are equipped with magnetic readers linked via the telephone system to banks and credit organizations. This is known as electronic funds transfer at point of sale (EFTPOS) and a shop using this system can instantly check that a card is valid and automatically debit the customer's account as each purchase is made.

EFTPOS systems are not always free of errors and faults. In order to try and overcome this some banks have experimented with plastic cards that have silicon chips built into them. Known as a 'smart card', this type of card has an electronic memory that keeps a record of transactions made and the amount of money in the user's account.

The information on a smart card can only be displayed at a cash dispenser. However, this problem has been solved with the latest type of smart card, which comes complete with a small LCD screen and touch-sensitive keyboard. A smart card is basically a small personal databank and in the future smart cards will probably be used for other purposes, such as holding a person's medical record.

Space exploration has done much to help the development of communications and computer technology. Controlling the Voyager 2 spacecraft as it flew past the planet Neptune in 1989 required highly sophisticated computers, and equipment capable of picking up signals several million times weaker than the power that it takes to operate an electronic watch.

Space communications began with the launch of the very first satellite, the Russian *Sputnik 1*, in 1957. Since then orbiting spacecraft have sent back increasingly complex signals. Today there are weather satellites, earth resources satellites and military satellites that transmit detailed pictures of the earth's surface 24 hours a day. These satellites can provide information that would be impossible to gather at ground level.

Landsat satellites produce images of the surface of the earth. These provide information about such things as natural resources, agriculture and pollution. This image shows San Francisco in California, USA. The false colours indicate different surface features.

The third and last Tracking and Data Relay Satellite (TDRS) being launched from the Space Shuttle *Discovery* in March 1989. The three TDRS satellites are in geostationary orbits and provide communications links between the ground, other satellites and spacecraft with astronauts working on board.

Even more remarkable are the pictures we have received from the interplanetary probes that have been sent out to nearly all of the planets in our Solar System. From these probes scientists have gathered fascinating information about Mercury, Venus, Mars, Jupiter, Saturn, Uranus and Neptune and their moons.

Satellite communications have also become an important feature of life here on planet Earth. One of the first communications satellites was the American *Echo 1*, which was launched in 1960 and acted like a giant orbiting radio reflector. More powerful transmissions were achieved with *Courier 1B*, which was launched by the US Army in the same year and carried equipment for boosting the signals it relayed.

The first public communications satellite was *Telstar*, launched in 1962. It relayed the first television pictures from the USA to Europe and could also carry up to 60 telephone calls at the same time. *Telstar* could only be used when its orbit brought it into a suitable part of the sky. The solution to this problem is to launch a satellite in such a way that it always remains above the same point on the ground. This is known as a geosynchronous, or geostationary, orbit and is achieved when the satellite orbits 35,880 km above the equator.

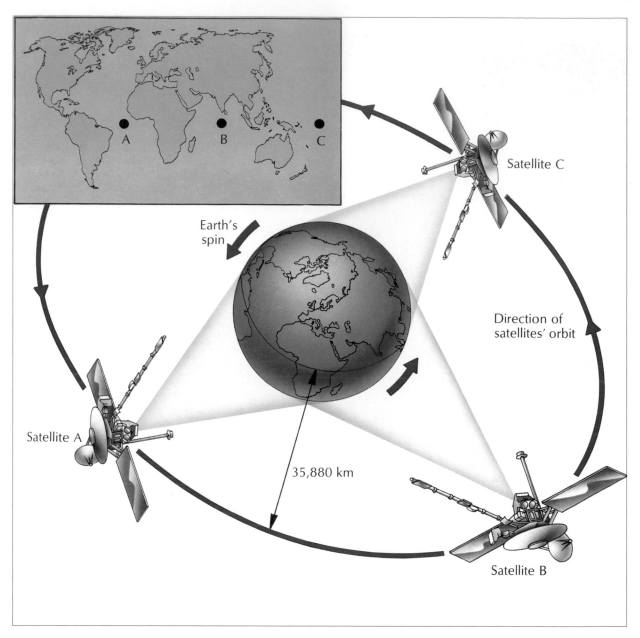

Earth's spin

Direction of satellites' orbit

Satellite C

Satellite A

Satellite B

35,880 km

A system of three geostationary satellites placed at equal distances from each other around the equator can be used to relay signals between any two points on earth.

Three such geostationary satellites, orbiting at equal distances from each other, are able to provide continual satellite communications throughout the world, by relaying signals to and from each other and stations on earth. The most modern communications satellites can each carry several thousand telephone calls as well as television pictures. Recently, satellites have been launched to transmit direct broadcast satellite (DBS) television signals beamed up to them from the ground. The signals are beamed down again directly into people's homes via dish-shaped aerials. In some cases the signals are scrambled so that they can not be 'read' until they have been unscrambled again using a special decoder.

Information technology has been playing a gradually increasing role in people's home life for over a hundred years – ever since the first telephone systems began to spread. Just look around your house today; you may be surprised at how many devices there are that process information electronically.

You may, for example, have a modern hi-fi system or radio-cassette player. The origins of these go back to 1877, when the American inventor Thomas Edison built a machine he called a phonograph for recording and reproducing sound on wax cylinders. The gramophone, which played flat records, was developed in the USA a few years later by Emile Berliner. Tape recording machines were invented during the 1930s, and when tape cassettes were developed in the 1960s the first hi-fi systems also began to appear. A modern hi-fi system may include a record player, a twin cassette tape recorder/player, a compact disc player and a tuner for receiving radio signals, all linked with amplifiers and speakers.

Elsewhere in your home there may be a television and a video recorder. Some of the latest televisions are equipped with digital technology that allows such things as freeze frame and picture in picture. Some video recorders can now be programmed using laser 'pens' and printed bar codes. The bar code indicates the channel and the start and stop times of the television programme.

The first sound recording system was invented by Thomas Edison in 1877. Sound vibrations were recorded by a needle tracing a wavy pattern in a piece of tin foil on the surface of a revolving drum. The recording could be played back using the same needle and a listening cone.

During the 1980s, microcomputers became popular for playing video games.

Your telephone may already be linked to one of the latest digital exchanges, which are more reliable than earlier ones and enable people to obtain dialled numbers more rapidly. Using digital technology, telephone companies are now offering a number of special services, such as three-way calling and call-diversion to another telephone number, that can be used simply by sending signals to the exchange by pressing buttons on the telephone.

Many people now own a home computer. Most are used for such things as playing games, helping with schoolwork, writing letters and doing household accounts. Computer enthusiasts also use them for writing programs and linking up, via the telephone system, with other computers. In the future, this ability to link up with the outside world is likely to make computers the most important part of information technology in the home.

Information has to be stored and processed in nearly every kind of business. Details of customers and suppliers must be filed away ready for use when required, information about products has to be stored, accounts must be kept and people have to be kept informed about what is going on. An office is an information centre and, not surprisingly, it is here that recent developments in information technology have had the greatest impact.

The essential features of an office are an information recording system, an information storage system and a message system. Up until two hundred years ago all information was recorded by hand and stored in ledgers or files. Messages had to be carried by hand from one office to another. Over the years technology has gradually improved the efficiency and speed of office systems.

The typewriter, invented in Italy in 1808, was the first machine to change the way people worked in offices. Typewriters started to become widely used during the late nineteenth century, with the result that letters and other documents could be produced more quickly. Typing became a new, socially acceptable occupation for women and thus it was the typewriter that first allowed women to become involved in office work.

Meanwhile, office communications were improving. Since the 1830s it had been possible to send messages over long distances using the electric telegraph. During the early twentieth century, subscriber telegraph services, such as the British telex and the American TWX systems, were introduced, and the transfer of information really began to speed up. At the same time the development of the telephone helped to make offices run more smoothly.

The typewriter, telephone and telex remained the main forms of office technology until the

Remington
Typewriters
DO THE WORK
WYCKOFF, SEAMANS & BENEDICT,
327 Broadway, New York.

An advertisement for one of the early Remington typewriters in 1900.

1960s. At this point computers began to be introduced into offices and the filing systems began to change. A large amount of the information that previously had been stored as paper documents could now be recorded on magnetic tape. Today, magnetic tape is still used in some large computers, but smaller computers use magnetic discs. The contents of a thick A4 file can be stored on a floppy disc measuring just 12.5 cm across, and a single hard disc can be used to store all the files of a small office. Using a keyboard and screen, the contents of magnetically stored files can be retrieved very quickly. Filing systems became known as information storage and retrieval systems.

The first electric typewriter was manufactured in 1902, but this type of machine did not become widely used until the 1960s. At about the same time photocopying machines, first developed in 1947, became more widespread. Various systems were tried out, but the one that is now most common uses light to create an electrically charged image on a metal drum or plate.

Below   In a photocopier, an electrical image is formed on a metal drum. This image attracts particles of carbon which are then transferred to paper

Above   A floppy disc is simply a thin, circular plastic disc coated with magnetic iron oxide. The surface can be easily damaged and a floppy disc is usually enclosed in a protective case or envelope.

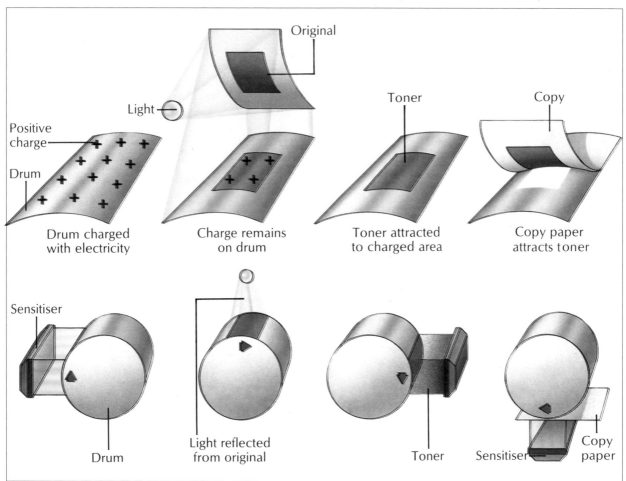

Original

Light

Positive charge

Drum

Drum charged with electricity

Charge remains on drum

Toner

Toner attracted to charged area

Copy

Copy paper attracts toner

Sensitiser

Drum

Light reflected from original

Toner

Sensitiser

Copy paper

A computer that is equipped with a word-processor program can be used to create and store text.

A fine black powder is attracted to this image, and is then transferred to a piece of paper. Today, there are also colour copiers, in which a document being copied is scanned three times, through different colour filters. The latest type of machine uses a laser to create the image on the printing drum.

Electric typewriters helped to speed up office work considerably. However, since the early 1980s they have begun to be replaced by computers programmed as word processors. Using this type of system, characters typed on to a keyboard are displayed on the computer screen instead of directly on to paper. It is therefore possible to make corrections and alterations before printing out the text via a computer printer. The text can also be stored on a magnetic disc.

The text for this book, for example, was written on a small computer, using a word-processor program specially created for the machine. At the publishers, the edited text was typed into another computer equipped with a desk-top publishing (DTP) program. The finalized text was stored on a magnetic disc, and this was used to help create the finished book. In theory, at least, it is possible to produce a book using computers alone, with the text being printed out only at the final stage. At present, however, publishers and writers still like to see 'hard' copy printed out on paper at least once during the publishing process.

In a modern office, computers are used for a range of different tasks, such as word processing, desk-top publishing, data storage and keeping accounts.

Computers are now an essential part of office life. A small computer, complete with keyboard, screen and often a printer, is an electronic workstation. It might well be linked into the telephone system and may form part of a whole network of workstations, all linked to a large, central computer.

The electronic workstation is thus a type-writer, filing system and communications centre all rolled into one. With this, a photo-copier and a fax machine, the high-tech office is complete. It does not even have to be in the same building as other offices in the same company. More and more people are working from their own homes. A home-based office can form part of a network in which many such offices are linked to each other and to a central office equipped with a mainframe computer.

Almost by definition factories are the home of technology. Every manufacturing process involves technology of one kind or another, and it is seldom long before industry finds ways of using new technologies. Information technology is no exception to this; computers and information systems are now an important part of many manufacturing processes.

Computers are often involved at the very start of a product's life. A computer-aided design and manufacturing, or CAD/CAM, system uses sophisticated graphics to enable designers to create two- or three-dimensional images on a screen, 'fit' parts together and draw fine detail on parts that will eventually be made too small for the human eye to see. Many things, from engines to cars and from silicon chips to complete computers are now designed in this way.

Once a part is designed, the instructions for making it can be programmed directly into a robot or a computerized machine tool. A robot is a machine equipped with one or more movable arms controlled by a computer 'brain'. Robots vary from simple types dedicated to performing just one task, to versatile machines that can be switched from one task to another almost instantly. Today's robots are used for such jobs as lifting, carrying, assembling, painting, welding, drilling, polishing and gluing. Future robots will have senses, such as vision and touch, that will enable them to be even more versatile.

Computers are used in the design and manufacture of electronic circuits.

Robots and other computer-controlled machines are an essential part of what is called a flexible manufacturing system, or FMS. This is a factory system designed to cope with manufacturing a wide variety of similar products in relatively small quantities, such as parts for aircraft. Computer-controlled machines are divided into groups, or cells. Each cell can produce a range of similar articles and can be rapidly reprogrammed to produce the particular one that is required.

In recent years factories have become highly automated. In a computer-integrated manufacturing, or CIM, system, the whole manufacturing process, from design and production planning to the manufacture of the finished article, is controlled by computers. Because computers manage the flow of information around the factory more efficiently than humans, a CIM system greatly speeds up the manufacturing process and helps to ensure a high level of quality control.

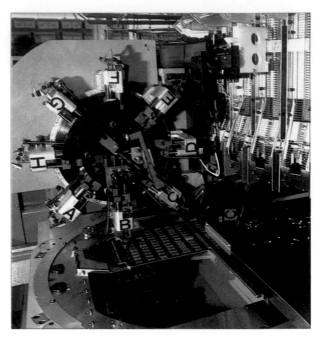

Above   In this factory, a specially designed robot selects silicon chips from a rotating dispenser and attaches them to printed circuit boards.

Today, computer-controlled welding robots are found in the assembly lines of all the manufacturers of mass-produced cars.

The information revolution seems set to continue, as more and more information has to be gathered, processed, stored and retrieved. Future computers will have to be faster and more powerful than the machines of today.

One way of achieving this may be to use superconducting materials – materials in which electricity flows freely because the electrical resistance is zero. Resistance decreases as the temperature of a material is reduced and some materials need cooling to almost impossibly low temperatures to achieve superconductivity. Tin, for example, has to be cooled to below $-269°C$, close to absolute zero, $-273°C$. However, scientists are now discovering 'warm' superconductors that work at relatively high temperatures. For example, one such material becomes a superconductor when cooled to $-148°C$.

Alternatively, future computers may process information using light beams travelling through air and optical fibres. Optical switches are also being developed, and eventually there may be completely optical computers that will work, quite literally, at the speed of light.

Computers of this type are likely to be very expensive at first and initially they will probably be used only for such things as scientific research and space exploration. Meanwhile, however, there are also plenty of possibilities in the more ordinary world. Silicon chip technology has now reached a point at which it is possible to produce amazingly powerful microprocessors and memory chips with huge capacities. Electronics companies are now making a whole range of small microprocessor-based devices, such as electronic personal organizers, databanks, dictionaries and language translators.

The usefulness of some of these devices is perhaps questionable, especially when they are

One of the key tests of a superconductor is that a magnetic field cannot penetrate it. A small magnet therefore floats above a piece of superconducting material. Here a scientist is demonstrating one of the new ceramic 'warm' superconductors, yttrium-barium-copper oxide.

compared in price to more conventional notebooks and printed dictionaries. But it is clear that electronics companies are urgently looking for ways of using the electronic technology they are creating.

Above   In January 1990 scientists at AT & T's Bell Laboratories in New Jersey, USA, headed by Alan Huang, shown here, announced that they had built the first experimental digital optical processor. If their research proves successful, it will be an important step towards the development of optical computers.

Below   The technology required to produce a video phone already exists, as is shown by this Japanese prototype. However, there is some doubt as to whether enough people will actually want such a device to make its manufacture worthwhile.

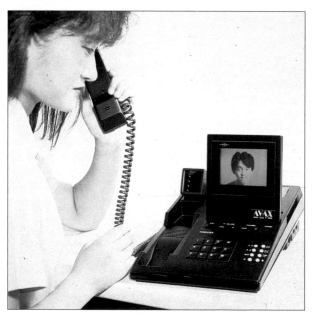

Data networks seem likely to spread and perhaps one day every business computer in the world may be linked into a global data network. People's homes may also form part of future data networks. Within the next twenty years or so it will probably become commonplace for people to have home-based computers that they can use for personal banking. Using such a system it will be possible to issue instructions to the bank's computer to pay bills and move funds between different accounts.

The same computer may also be used for ordering goods from the local supermarket, booking theatre or airline tickets and sending messages to friends. It will also form part of a completely integrated home communications and control system. This will monitor and control such things as the heating, electrical and alarm systems. It will even be possible to issue instructions to the computer from anywhere in the world by telephone, using both the telephone keypad and a voice recognition system.

In this way the computer could be instructed by the user to do such things as draw the curtains and switch on lights to deter intruders, turn the heating up and start cooking the evening meal.

Future computers are likely to be cleverer than those of today. A great deal of work is now being done, particularly in Japan, on the development of a new generation (the so-called 5th generation) of computers. The intention is that these will be intelligent computers that can learn in much the same way as we do, deduce facts and ideas, and be able to communicate with humans. The study of control and communication in machines and animals is known as cybernetics. Cyberneticists hope one day to be able to improve the way we communicate with computers, perhaps by finding ways of linking human brains directly with computer circuits.

In the distant future, brand new technologies may be developed. As we attempt to store and process more and more information, we will wish to do so in an ever smaller amount of space. At present the smallest electronic devices can be viewed using a powerful microscope. But it is possible to envisage information storage devices that consist of just one or two molecules of material.

At this point, of course, we are starting to enter the realms of science fiction. But sometimes science fiction becomes science fact.

Individual transistors and their connections can be seen on the surface of a silicon chip by viewing the surface through a scanning electron microscope. In the future electronic devices may be even smaller.

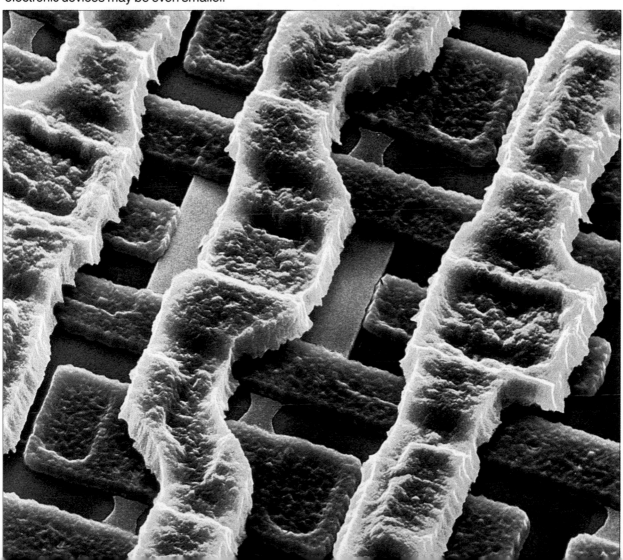

Glossary

Absolute zero. The lowest temperature that it is theoretically possible to reach; −273.15°C.

Analogue system. A system, such as a computer, telephone or radio, in which information is represented by continuously varying electrical signals.

Cable television. A television signal supplied to the viewer via an electrical or optical fibre cable.

Capacitor. An electrical device that stores electric charge.

Cathode ray tube. A device for generating a beam of electrons (cathode rays) and focussing it on to a fluorescent screen.

Chip. An abbreviated form of microchip or silicon chip.

Database. A computer program designed for the storage and retrieval of information.

Databank. A computer permanently programmed with a database.

Data network. A network of computers linked via cables, such as those of the telephone system.

Digital system. A system in which information is converted into a form that represents numbers, or digits.

Diode. An electrical device with two electrodes that converts alternating current into direct current.

Electrode. A conductor by which electricity enters or leaves a device such as a diode, triode or electric cell (battery).

Electronic. Concerned with the fine control of very small electric currents.

Facsimile transmission. A system used for sending reproduced copies of documents via the telephone system or by radio.

Fax. An abbreviation of facsimile.

Floppy disc. A magnetic computer storage disc consisting of a flexible piece of plastic covered with a thin film of iron oxide.

Graphics program. A computer program designed to produce pictures on a screen.

Hard disc. A magnetic computer disc consisting of a rigid piece of plastic covered with a thin film of iron oxide. It is designed to hold more information than a floppy disc and the information is read by a special head that floats on a thin layer of air above the disc. The disc and head are encased in an airtight container to keep out dust.

Hieroglyphics. An ancient form of written language that used picture symbols to represent objects and ideas.

Hi-fi. An abbreviation for high-fidelity, used to describe high-quality sound-reproducing equipment.

Laser. A device that produces a very intense, pure, parallel beam of light.

Light-emitting diode (LED). A form of semiconductor diode that gives out light as an electric current passes through it.

Liquid crystal display (LCD). A flat screen that uses special crystals and polarized light to display digits, characters or images.

Mainframe computer. A large, powerful computer.

Microchip. A silicon chip.

Microwave. A high frequency, very short wavelength radio wave.

Optical fibre. A thin strand of glass constructed in such a way that light passes along it without escaping from the side.

Optical fibre cable. A cable containing one or more optical fibres.

Personal computer. A small desk-top computer complete with screen, keyboard and, usually, a printer.

Radio. A form of communication that uses radio waves which travel through space without the need for wires.

Radio telephone. A telephone system in which speech is transmitted partly by radio and partly by wires.

Rectifier. A diode.

Resistance. A measure of the extent to which a material resists the flow of an electric current. When resistance is high, current flow is low.

Resistor. A device that resists the flow of an electric current.

Semiconductor. A material with the basic properties of a non-conductor of electricity that can, under the right conditions, be made to act as a conductor.

Silicon chip. An integrated circuit. A thin slice of silicon on which have been placed a number of electronic devices together with their interconnections.

Smart card. A plastic data or credit card containing a silicon chip.

Telegraph. A method of communication that involves sending coded electrical signals along a wire.

Telephone. A device or system used to transmit speech along a wire.

Teletex (supertelex). A telegraph system, operated over telephone lines and designed to link computers, particularly those being used as word processors.

Teletext. Computer-stored information broadcast by television companies at the same time as ordinary television signals.

Telex. The British form of modern telegraph system operated via the telephone network.

Transistor. A semiconductor triode.

Triode. An electrical device with three electrodes that can be used to amplify an electrical signal or as an electronic switch.

Viewdata. Computer-stored information that can be sent via the telephone network and viewed on a television screen or computer monitor.

Word processor. A computer program designed to enable the user to write and manipulate text on a screen before it is printed out. The term is also used to describe a computer being used for this purpose or a computer that is designed to do nothing else.

Further reading

Ardley N, *Computers* (Kingfisher, 1983)
Blackburn D and Holister G, *Encyclopedia of Modern Technology* (Hutchinson, 1987)
Lambert M, *TV and Video Technology* (Wayland, 1989)
Lambert M, *20th Century Communications* (Wayland, 1988)

Lambert M, *50 Facts about Electronics* (Piper Books, 1984)
Myring L and Graham I, *Information Revolution* (Usborne, 1983)
Nicholls P (Ed.), *The Science in Science Fiction* (Michael Joseph, 1982)
How is it Done? (Reader's Digest, 1990)

Index

Picture Acknowledgements

The publishers would like to thank the following for allowing their photographs to be reproduced in this book:
Ann Ronan Picture Library 6, 7, 11, 33, 35; Eye Ubiquitous *front cover*, 28 (above); Mark Lambert 15 (above); Sainsbury's 28 (below); Science Photo Library 5 (above), 12, 14, 15 (below), 16, 17, 19 (both), 23, (above), 24, 26, 27, 30, 31, 34, 36 (above), 38, 39, 40 (below), 41, 43; Sony (UK) 10; Telefocus 13 (both), 21; Topham 4, 8, 9, 20, 42 (both); Wayland Picture Library 18, 23 (below), 25, 37; ZEFA 5 (below), 40 (above).
Artwork by the Hayward Art Group.